The Canopy

Also by Patricia Clark

Sunday Rising
She Walks into the Sea
My Father on a Bicycle
North of Wondering

Chapbooks
Wreath for the Red Admiral
Given the Trees

For Tracy K. Smith —
in admiration
for all you do
for poetry!

The Canopy

Patricia Clark
Patricia Clark

Terrapin Books

Terrapin Books
4 Midvale Avenue
West Caldwell, NJ 07007

www.terrapinbooks.com

ISBN: 978-0-9976666-4-9
LCCN: 2016958602

First Edition

Cover art: *Steller's Jay*, oil on canvas, by Stanley Krohmer

for my sister
Kathleen Gehrt
1946-2014

Contents

III

I'm by all waters now.

—Theodore Roethke

Knives on the Irish Air

Today, twice, from whispering leaves, a voice—
enough so I turned around,

my long look stroked the lawn, my lashes
made a willow's long branch,

no suggestion yet of breakage or a cry,
and the window's eye blinked.

The cry, though, came again, forming
around a name, my sister's name,

then gone. It's something I'm giving up
to live in the morning air, this

leaf-listening, the sister-worrying.
Now I'll take myself to lake and rocky shore,

in Irish air, any air, and breathe,
letting the knife settle where it will,

blade nestled between a rib and a rib.

I

Balance, January

It's stranger than you can account for,
being alive, a cold January morning and twenty
wild turkeys high up in white oaks,
their waking up stretches in half-light—
first unbending out of a hunched ball, then
unfurling a wing, the second, while the broad
tail sticks out, flares, judders up and down.
Everyone says how stupid they are, will drown
when it rains simply by gazing up. I can't
call them beautiful—but I grudgingly give them
credit for the way they balance on brittle thin
branches seemingly without fear. How to have
poise, to nestle down to rest on a fragile thing?

Frontal View of Trees

after Wolf Kahn

I like it when the trunks
                of the birches
         take up earth's
      mantis green,
that's what she would do—
                appropriate the ground,
        by sinking in.

She troubles me, my mother
                who didn't die
         comforted, at home.
      Our bodies point to fates
we live but cannot decipher.
                The sun offers
        its warming touch.

Souls of the dead, thin
                presences and pale—
         yet their spirits
      have turned to light—
glow of cumin, cinnamon ruddy
                in the corner
        of the canvas.

To misread means to author
                your own text—
         in truth, the trunks
      wear flood marks, mud

floating high in water left
                    the smear.
          She fell down.

Smack of the ground's kiss,
                 that broke
          her nose. The doctor said,
dead before she hit the ground.
Linked once, she and I severed now
                    and who will be
          at my side when I go?

The birches make a grove
                   collecting light—
          she wore a verve
      for living, cloak
of many colors.

Vertigo

The world unhinged, aswirl, a tent uprooted—
stakes pulled out, sides billowing,
floor heaving,

just pulling on a shirt or looking up—
soaping my hair, streams of water tumbling
in the shower,

awful realization, each eye flick, head
movement connects to the stomach's
uneasy sea,

oh ocean-sick sailor, how will you board
the tanker for the next port, or climb
a mast? To walk

the room, I must hold on, not sure
where to plant right foot—then left—
grip, and clutch the wall.

How soon the stable world vanishes
for tilt, unsteady, sheer dread uncertainty,
yesterday remembered as granite floor.

The Prodigal Daughter

Now comes rainy May, gray skies, tulips laden with weeping.
Saw a weasel step across the grass.
First, there was a bronze hummingbird,
                          then the weasel turning its head.

In the tide pools, blood star—with its thin arms—
                    and red California sea cucumber.

No music after ten p.m.
Sparrows silent except for rustling in the hemlock,
                      whisper and wink of salmonberry.

My Mother's Voice

High and muddy flecked with white
                    fluff from cottonwoods,

that's the river slipping by this morning,
                    my walk taking me deep and long.

Some mornings I imagine walking
                    forever, into the city, back.

A regular crew of people stroll here, then
                    disappear—I still recall

Nola, who was going blind, her black dog
                    Cody—it's been a couple years

since they came here. The second day
                    of Ramadan—I hear this announced

on the news—the faithful fasting all day
                    then the joyful meal shared at dusk.

We used to fast on Sundays before
                    swallowing those Communion wafers

at Visitation or St. Teresa's, and on Friday nights, no
                    roasted flesh, ate fish instead.

A hike into the city, back, what jive
                    is that? I live here already.

Saturdays she'd announce, "We're cleaning
                    house—put that book down!"

There's a whole world out there, river's
                    the moving, secret source.

"Who do you think you are?" she'd say,
                    "Don't be so high and mighty!"

Hardwoods

after Larkin's "Water"

If I were called in
to construct a religion
based on what's at hand,
I would make use of trees.

Some rituals could involve
lying at their feet in wonder,
detecting color variation
as examples, in green alone,

of God's variety of grace.
Stripping naked, a baptismal
rite, would involve being tied
to a trunk, standing through rain.

We could try grouping up under
their boughs in prayer, hearing
sighs in wind, the soughing cry
of ecstasy or remembered pain.

Couples in training for marriage
would practice grafting, the slender
cut, insertion of a wood sliver, then
binding with tape to see what grows.

Imagining last rites would mean
deadwood under bite of saw
or the axe, the curative mysteries
lent by fire, then rising smoke.

Resurrection always takes place
at dawn, gray, decomposing leaf scent
mixing with the uplift of ash,
lake effect snow, voices saying my name.

Milkweed Pod

It's the boat I choose
for transport
into the new year

I lie down in its hammered
gold, my right
shoulder against
its curve

From this posture, I will study
stars, meteors,
Milky Way and any way

I trust to its rough
bark, gray, textured
like a mouse's ear—
waterproof, seam split

Reaching up, I touch
a furled sail
of seeds, sleeping

Do you note the light
changing along the river?
Already it seeps in—
lifting hem of this,

edge of seed, fur
of seedpod shell and stem—
set adrift, alight

Come My Cantillations

Come my cantillations,
let us bundle together and tie with string,
white kitchen twine, the messy package of our fears,
mailing them off to another address,
let me be free of invoices,
let me be free of leash laws at the park,
let come together beautiful thoughts,
thoughts in clean sentences scrubbed of excess,
thinking canvas, paint, the brush, the line,
let come makers with their smocks, spattered wrists,
let come wisdom from lifting a hand,
let come spark-glints in their eyes.
I speak of open spaces, wrought surfaces,
of clarity like gusty air, blowing the window wide.

Treatise on the Double Self

The Irish swallows take
        risks, swooping under, around
    the black picnic table,
            curving up
   near windows, shuttered,
then out to the tree circled by wire,
         solo on the lawn,
   banking around to start again.

Low in grass, a scattering
        of buttercups and companions,
   the ox-eye daisies,
          making a galaxy
   beneath our feet replacing sky,
invisible, obscured.
         No rain at the moment,
  a blessing, everything's soaked, dripping.

Here's the double self, the one now,
        the other of nine years ago,
   did you see her white face
          from the window,
   or catch a glimpse of her shoulder
turning the corner, hallway meeting hall?
        That's the woman
   who had a mother then,

a hill of trees, then a field
        sloping green and shorn down
   to the lake's edge—that's how
         this heart is, landscape

revealing where we've been and are.
Yesterday three times a bird sounded
                its cry from pines—
staying hidden, not swooping out

like the swallows. Wet, I stopped in woods,
         listening, wanting to see
     its shape, was it dove, or pied
                flycatcher? My attention
   went to the hidden one—
I've spent hours and months trying to know
        my mother.

Land of Getaway

They are bones, tomorrow,
who were our friends.

This in the land of getaway,
a lake cabin on loan,

where I wake out of a dream,
the bed as coffin,

where a blue moon lays down
its wide milkiness,

and curtain panels, sky blue
and white, billowed,

then clapped shut.
The bright gold seaplane

lands skimming like a damselfly
near fishermen dropping lead

from pontoon boats, trying
to go deep. It's not

a day for mourning—in flats,
bedding plants wait—

thirsty, of one season only,
aching toward the light.

Double Vision

Nine long years ago I had a mother,
            today these words tolling like a bell
      near Lake Annaghmakerrig,
                        this valley and drumlin hills,
      ringing a soft lament over fields
I walked in rain, in sun,
            not thinking of her then
      not knowing as I do now
                        in bones, fiber, skin,
what a body takes, then leaves.

When a fine misty rain shivers down
            over pasture, walkways, lawns
      dotted with buttercups,
                        it's almost time to walk again,
      taking a lane that skirts the lough.
It's where I spied the red fox—
            glimpsed twice now,
      mid-stride in surprise,
                        a live gray thing
struggling from its mouth to get away.

Artisan

after Nicholas Samaras

I make this room a country
of flowers, winter demands it,

broken trees, frozen ground
speaking of the grave, a terrible diction

I refuse to learn. It's fair, I think,
to long for what refuses us—

the moss green of new growth, delicate
blossoms in balloon or ray shapes.

I make this room a country of petals—
the gallica rose in its fuchsia

extravagance, repeat blooming into August.
I make this room a country of shelter,

roof and floor a steady pledge from the safe,
walls the very symbol of sentinels.

I make this room a country for those
sent away, the one from Wylie Street,

lover of horses and words, and an Irish
writer, his narrow kind face,

a clerk at sixteen, a laboring lad,
and *not* my sister, one who fast-walks

eight miles around her city a day,
not going anywhere. I demand an end

to this cataloging, this dreaded leave-
taking. Instead, I make this room my

country of astringent light, trying to craft
out of cold air an enlightening brew,

aiming to create with lamenting words, deep
sorrow, an invigorating heel-kicking tune.

Nakedness, Spared

When errands take you out into the world,
        when you feel your body tugged, pulled again,
when the cream line milk you bought
        comes thick and rich in glass bottles
and the milk's color is not white
        but ivory, with palest gold in it
like a cloud with the sun behind it,
        when you shower, feeling all the dust
of several months washing off, swirling
        away down the drain, what does it mean,
after all, to strip down to essentials?
        Skin, water, spirit, the light of dusk
coming on now, and you're called to join
        your lover in bed, touching, kissing, licking—
purity of desire making the room
        dissolve, both losing track of time—
and what a strange thing it is, rolling
        together with this man, how well,
ever, do we know another person,
        going on together to bare what is
intimate, see us now in all
        our nakedness, the way you wept
when the dog's life was spared, rescued
        from the road by a stranger,
and the dog lay exhausted on the slate
        floor, all of us saved,
no one unaccounted for, night
        coming on, the moon's silver sickle
tipping like a brittle ornament.

Sword Fern

From the tall stalk, from Puget lowlands,
this long frond coping to unwind—
scrolled at the tip end, treble clef, tail

of the magical seahorse. My mare,
sister, let us step lightly on spongy ground
into May's landscape where moss lies down,

inching forward. I don't want to lift swords,
contending, vying. If we spar, I fear
the blade at my throat, its tip

at my eyeball—you are quick beyond
all telling, I cannot help but shy
from you. What does it mean to share

blood, root-hairs? I am at a loss
to know. Is a chorus frog snugged
at your base? Let us make

shelter for the new singing ones, not
fighting but saying softly, tell, let in, in
where most tender, gentle, and most soft.

Cottage at the Lake: Two Views

i.

Dew on lawn chairs and canvas
beads of it on the grass,
how your feet leave tracks—

so still, a fire cracks, a phoebe whistles—

is there any "now what?"

Surely these are the brief times—so let's
kick up our heels—

I thought of dancing—
pushing the furniture back to the walls.

A boat growls and pulls the skier up.

ii.

This is a slow hour
             Carolina wren on the railing

man on the dock in a folding chair
             summer after summer.

The lake's a gull wing
             blue streaks of waves.

Our dog fell in the water
　　　but knew, instinctively, to paddle.

What do we know like that?
　　　　　I turn to you—finding
the body's shore, ladder of spine.

Lamentation

On the phone we exchange night visions of her,
our departed red-headed sister. In Dan's lucky dream
she tells him "good work," patting his hand.

In mine, she's a head lying on the floor, a thing the dog
sniffs until I jerk the leash. Jean scrubs carpet:
"We're divvying up silverware. Want some?"

In another dream, I walk the street, our old neighborhood,
asking for money, hand held out at the Torbas—always
so kind—like trick or treat, souling, eve of All Souls.

Thus does so much become ash, her wishes, too,
like ash, all the smudges on our foreheads
those long-ago Wednesdays, when we knelt

devout in earnest, not knowing yet in church
those weekday mornings before school, just why
coffins were there, and why we sang.

II

Clark

after Weldon Kees

The maintenance man calls himself Fred,
calls these buildings "suds" because as Clark notes down
the laundry folks lived here, washing clothes,
and more, for the officers on the base.

"Where's the shutoff valve?" –but no one knows.
Fred will check a map; Clark drives away.
The music tears a ragged hole into her heart.

When the battleship gray clouds match walls
someone better go out, go dance and forget.
There are maps in the car, sand on the floor.
There's a coastline eroding with the tide, so go.

Flowers to buy: no more pale tulips, but blooms
like dahlias, spiky, nodding, in neon
shades of red, purple, gold. "Tender" the word

for dahlias, Clark recalls from the green thumb
woman—her mother, if the name be known.

Outside, the birds crank up cries like jazz.
Outside, the four suds buildings make a square.
Where the bay glints pewter and takes no prisoner.

After Lightning

I am the bright sliver of wood
thrown like a spear into the ground.
Where white-tails step past

there are signs of their passing.

And also the red-tailed hawk on the woodpile,

the rustlings of prey: chipmunk, whiskered mouse.

I am the creek that meanders
behind these houses. Watershed hidden in ravines,
unnamed. Like secret tears,
I soften, flow. Movement

instead of stasis. A sparkling
silver like a necklace thrown off.

I am the chorus of peepers
surprising ears after winter's hard
silence. When the oaks

join in with their rustling,
a layer of sound goes on top,
varnish, a clear coat. I am

the mysterious offering of a hand
to the one who turned away.
And the delphinium bloom with a black eye.

The heart of a sister—
a sister's hardened heart.

What word would I say?

Demonifuge

And so I lifted the cup
                and held it lip to lip

drank it down, mostly
                      in one draught. Taste?

Plum, blackberry, soot,
                and mauve oak leaf.

I stood alone, facing out
                    through trees, the way people

stand at the shore, a hem
                of surf touching their toes.

My desire was sharp
                in my belly, ache of

appendix or kidney stone.
                Let the demon go! I

urged, and when I turned,
                    setting the goblet on a rotting log

I saw at its bottom
                grains of stuff like

crystals or flakes, horny
                scales of a departing beast.

Fragrant Cigar Boxes

The objects, in one day, become junk.
That is, treasures on a desk—
a broken pale pink shell, a mottled stone picked up
near Lake Superior.

Does nothing, then, hold inherent value?

My mother saved coffee grounds,
eggshells.

It wasn't easy to cook a meal in her kitchen.
Were the dishwasher dishes clean,
or dirty? Was a cracked bowl by the faucet
one of those loved things?

In the world, there is also trash.
The used up, spent, crumpled, worn.

Words spoken on an island: I promise
to hold you until the end. I promise not
to leave your side.

Though it had rained all night, what is called
a "bucketing rain" in Ireland, though
streams of it ran down the trunks of oaks,
still this whole vertical part of one trunk stayed
dry as bone.

I remember playing with acorns, laying them
down like children, in cigar boxes—
fragrant ones from my grandfather.

Some even slept in their caps.

Postcard Painting

Wanted to believe I was shrinking—
        could slip into the space
     behind ochre paint
          where some dark figure—
      perhaps a large boat,
   lay obscured.

That headland beyond—
      and streaked sky
   shedding rain.

Shadow of the Lightning-Struck Tree

Still upright, not trembling, and casting yet
    a length of dark in the ravine

though it was not blackened by the bolt,
    nor set afire, just rent,

and its living wood, heartwood, was split
    to spear-lengths, thrown

into the arms of other nearby trees, pierced
    a few inches into soft ground.

A friend said look for fulgurite
    at its foot—how lightning's heat

transforms wet sand. I never could
    go down there, stepping onto spongy

earth, bending and mosquito-bitten, to see,
    not wanting to touch the open place

where bark tore, pale tender cambium
    living, splintery, a chest exposed.

Someone in our city once called cottonwoods
    dirty, suggesting cutting them all down.

From up along the ridge I hear the whine
    a chainsaw makes, a neighbor man

cleaning up some brush. How will it stand,
    surviving winter months, wide

open to the ache of cold? I imagine years
    ahead, seeing half of it shorn

of leaves, the other half full, standing,
    swaying, its trunk creaking, seeming

to speak as it moves, play of light
    and dark, not a word finally said.

Pierced

Janice was my friend, junior high,
who lived in a rental house. Another

friend warned me—there's something
wrong with that place.
And maybe her, too.

When she moved away, there was no goodbye.

My brother Michael was a baby then.
The Sound of Music was all the rage.
We danced with him

singing, "High on the hill was a lonely
goatherd." None of us could yodel.

Before my friend moved, she pierced

my ears with darning needles, after
I held two ice cubes to the lobes.

The holes are still there—
I touch them every day.

Today a Snowstorm Caught Me Up

Today a snowstorm caught me up, heading home,
and I skidded through it. Which way is up?

The hills and intersections laid icy tracks,
my fingers gripped the wheel. My blood heated up.

The thrill of being alive, outcome unknown.
Or is it known? In dreams, she calls me up.

If I could sit at her side, lean in, talk about years
when our lives didn't intersect, and lift her up.

To have the mind give way because of cells
gone wild. It's wrong and it's snarled up.

The enemy: our bodies (skin and bone), or time?
We're racing against the clock. Is time up?

With each hour of a passing day, she goes farther
away, through drifting snow. Make her stand up!

Aerodynamic

Possibly sugar maple—
      this whirligig, samara, seed bearing
            bundle that sends
      DNA from the tree
out in the world to grow again.

Green-loaded weight-
      bearing on one end, split to show
    an escape's in progress.

Its other end's a wing, flat
    bottom, curved top,
        in shades of tan, an edge
chartreuse or lime, depending on the light.

How one flies, descends, like
      a fallen leaf, an object beautifully lean.
    When today's walk brings you
out past the tall prairie grass,

and bedstraw, bloodroot—where hardwoods
      send a trill of notes liquid
        as rain from a singer hidden, you wonder,
can it be warbler, oriole?

      You must listen beyond
    yourself, become part sylvan, verdant,
breathing, swaying, there.

After *The Lunchbox*

He lamented his crowded country, the man
            with soulful eyes in the movie.
"I had to buy a burial plot where I'll be standing up."

This morning I raised up the two-foot splinter
            from the lightning-struck tree

to save a black and white bumble bee on the porch,
            using this wood as my wand.

From what I've seen, it helps to keep
            a handkerchief handy.

Leaf-mounds heaped in the ravine
            buried another from last year

and the year before. We'll be coming back as
            mulch, my brother,
whether standing up or lying down.

My *Aberglaube*

Certain names and faces refuse to fade—
my mother in the living room her cheeks wet,
the news announcer saying the priest had been killed
by a drunk driver; and a pale girl in grade school,
Mary Fink, her house looped inside with streamers
for a party no one in my class went to except for me—
The day Bob Nelson pressed me up against a car
O wet exchange of tongues thrill of him hard
against me. The Youth Dew perfume my sister Jean
said would attract boys. Dresses I wore, one
with small polka dots, a shirtwaist, blue.
All Tacoma, gray forgotten streets, the hills where
the Chevy lost its brakes 6th Ave, K Street—
Belief in those beyond the certain and verifiable.

Where Rivers Cross

Think leaf, maple of course—
or starfish clinging to the pier,
underwater, coral-red.

The hand goes on working
in light, darkness, chill—
yesterday swinging a hammer,
knocking in the post
to steady the young redbud.

At the park, the hand
double-gloved. Still,
it must flex to keep warm.

Asking questions of its
opposite—

Will you help add an equal force?

Can you sub for me on day's
third shift so I can lie down?

The left works on
bicep curls, kickbacks.

Four fingers and a thumb
linked by a fertile plain—

Look where the rivers cross—
Count which ones make it
to the sea.

Even the smallest
tributary leaves a mark
in skin.

The flexible hand
remembers each
object held—

feather, shell, the apple
warm from another's hand.

Fatal Sentence

after listening to Philip Glass's Tirol Concerto

Each day it does not come
I raise my eyes
to the cottonwood's eighty-foot top,

saying, "Praise be."
Our end, then,
foreshadowed by being born,

but not forecast, yet.
Studying a wild turkey
parading in its feathered

finery--"glad rags" my father
used to call Sunday best--
I see through glass how it goes,

head jutting forward, crossing
Lamberton Creek, stepping
relentless as a clock, east.

Leaves just out on honeysuckle,
oak, mayapple spreading wide
its spoked umbrellas.

Our ends, foreshadowed by
being born, once, but not
forecast yet, oh air

that I gulp, turkey I bless
now walking west—awkward
along the creek's high bank.

Butte

A butte is a mesa's orphan. . .

To be the orphan means
feeling wind, then pelting rain

eroding half your mass. I want
to throw a shadow says the butte.

In the shade of my side
a herd of antelope might shelter.

I miss being part of my
mother mesa—I saw her

chipped away by those
curious at climbing, others

who built nests in her cliff-
face. Where there had grown

grass, it turned to bare dirt
becoming a river of silt.

Forlorn is what the wind says.
A sister butte nearby

and no way to build a natural
bridge from here to there.

The wind wailing past,
dust kicked up, whorls and whirls.

in memoriam Ellen Meloy

My Sister's Hand in Mine

Not one without the other, shimmer of water
        where the heron stands, mud dusted
    with pollen, a few downy duck feathers,

tracks where the night possum came out
        food-searching, found a few
    freshwater clams. Cracked shells

lie abandoned here, sucked dry, and there's shit
        everywhere, too, green and black
    coils from Canada geese.

Why sing of a ravaged spot at the Grand River
        needing dredging to clear
    silt out, so water will flow?

The whole place tangled and gross with invasive
        species—especially purple
    loosestrife, that looks elegantly tall

but crowds out bloodroot, spring beauty, the low
        ephemerals. In other places,
    poison ivy circles cottonwood, sycamore.

The heron lifts off, emits a squawk as sun
        smears up full, and boys come
    walking, sometimes throwing rocks,

"Can you hit that bird?" I would save her
        if I could, my sister beginning
    to forget some words and names.

Fig, Strawberry

It's best to taste the jam
　　　over many days, learning how
　　　　　to pick out the dark note
　　　of fig next to strawberry,
　　　　　　　　　letting your tongue
　　　and taste buds
　　　　　take you to Hungary, Moravia,

places she will not travel to now.
　　　You will have to go
　　　　　for your sister, standing in an orchard
　　　in Greece, walking there,
　　　　　　　　　the breba crop with the year's
　　　first figs, and then the main crop
　　　　　ripening more slowly.

You'll learn about the fig wasp
　　　needed for pollination—
　　　　　from its sting, its burrowing
　　　into the crown, then the crawl
　　　　　　　　　along the inflorescence,
　　　till it pollinates some of the female
　　　　　flowers, lays eggs, dies.

Strawberries grow differently, home raised
　　　in rows, and Mother took us
　　　　　to U-pick fields when we were
　　　children—often it's good to be
　　　　　　　　　low to the ground, getting down
　　　on your knees, not minding the dirt,
　　　　　working to uncover the last, sweet ones.

Columbus Day Storm

for Claudio Parmiggiani

The idea of art   as smoke, images left
by dark tendrils twining   after flame, the Italian
artist who burns tires,   piles of rubber in a room
to capture what remains,   smudge on white walls. She
took shape, then, a girl   straddling a bicycle, 1962,
after the windstorm, how   she rose to light, a house
of sleepers, no electricity,   and went out into streets
blocked by fallen trees,   saw a place transformed,
and she the Captain Cook,   Captain Vancouver to log
it all while her brothers   slept. Where power lines
sparked, she knew to leave   them alone, vowing to cross
danger, to note it crisply,   block to block, before
returning to fill their   astonished ears, having
the thrill of both—venturing out   alone, and then to tell.

III

The Canopy

In truth, Cloverdale Road doesn't end, blacktop
　　　giving way to packed Michigan dirt,
　　　　　　dark brown, unrutted, and the car's
　　　tires keep humming, it's just the tune
riffing, something I listen for.
　　　　　　　　The trees all dripping.

Come spring, the waited-for season, the woods
　　　reveal their true business, layer welcoming
　　　　　　the next, as first the forest floor
　　　blooms, then subsequent layers, bush,
　　　　　small sapling, up and up to
　　　　　　　　white oak, American beech.

They call wildflowers that come back
　　　spring ephemerals. Their time of bloom
　　　　　　in sequence before the canopy
closes, dark, impenetrable. The list
　　　grows long—wood anemone,
　　　　　　　blue cohosh, great waterleaf—

on and on, in columns, alphabetical, not listed
　　　by common name but by family.
　　　　　　Thus, the anemone group.
Blue cohosh joins the caulophylum
　　　members. No surprise that waterleaf, both
　　　　　　Virginianum and the great,

belong to the hydrophyllum group.
　　　Today, driving through downpours, rain
　　　　　　lashing at times, and now, walking,
　　　I note how brief the time allowed for them,
for us, light, air, vertical space to thrive in,
　　　　　　　before the canopy closes.

After the Ice Storm

On this day, the trees let loose
their burdens, fallen crystal
cracking into segmented pieces
across snow.

If there were occasion for
weeping, now nearly forgotten,
it came before freezing.

Now, the melting—solving
nothing. Thaw won't heal
where limbs cracked or failed,

where weight could crush,
and did.

Goodbye to the Poetry of Marble

after James Wright

Mother of arctic chill and tombs,
you have not bred coldness into our bones'
marrow. Despite the rolling pin, the cutting board,
marble may aid with pie dough, not so much
with a tender breast. I prefer to let
my spongy heart flex, tremble, hurt
for my sister. Let go your grip on me,
Sorrow. Let us lift up, celebrate and seize
what we might. Look how we honor, gather
to bend with care, refuse to abandon her.
This bond deeper than blood, stone.
The sight of needles, bandages makes
me dream of escape. Sower of discord,
disturber of nerve endings, brother of coal,
sister of scabs, let others offer their
litanies like jewels. Look how unworthy
I have become. I cannot even find
wax to stop up my ears.

The Slit

Thought I saw, at the day's start,
            a door open in an oak tree—
a vertical slit, a magical port—
                a figure stood there,
then disappeared—
           I could neither follow
        nor lie about the journey.

See how the light fills chamber and halls
            in the woods here?
The suggestion makes a church,
                narthex, nave, a place
for worship if you trust
         where your eyes
      take you, up and up.

Thought I knew when a leaf stood still
           something mirrored there,
the margin, toothed, irregular,
              and the oblong shape
      with veins spreading out like streams,
         where an estuary fills,
drains, makes a birthing place.

Where I did not lie down, a forest floor
           of mayapple, trillium, moss.
Birdcall of blue jay came with a laugh,
              others unidentified—
      one a phrase curling up
        at the end like sword fern,
then down, phrase two complete. Wood thrush?

Imagined I glimpsed, in light indistinct and fogged
                    with time, a door in a white oak
crack open, close, the way a cell
                    changes or allows a thing
        in—an ort of food, speck
                of water for the tree's throat,
bit of DNA ragged, flawed.

Someone ascended, believe if you will,
                a winding stair with no handrail,
found a place within, staying,
                    never emerging,
        a woodsy sequestering with bark,
                    duff for insulation—
breathing silence, rustling, watching beyond words.

This is for the Snow Drifting Down

like flour and for the way it cruises sideways
which is a sign for wind, also a sign

for cardinal directions, changeable as the bird
and able to craft a song though it is not

chew, chew like the red one itself but more
a whistle or a moan. This is for extreme cold

that burrows into teeth, gums, bones like snow
electrified, snow made into needles of pain.

This is for the heron stalking in creek mud
for a meal—I wish you luck, bird!

Minnow, vole, or frog—swallow it whole,
leave off stalking the rest of the snowy day.

This is for a new month, the great spin
of a roulette wheel turning—isn't that what

we're on?—And I call out for S in the night,
or he mutters for me. Twining vines, that's

what we are, holding on like English ivy,
this is for that fasthold, tentacle, grip.

My Sister's Earth Day

That it was Earth Day and still the leading
edges of an iceberg fell into the sea with a hiss,
the center showing pocked ice.

And the plane that had flown us home
parked, taxied, and flew again.

From a distance, the remote camera had an eye
in her death room. It was our way
of holding her, can you see it?

That a tree flowered outside her room—
planted for her daughter, blooming pink each year.

That it comes in waves—the crashing rain,
the pains in her head, the grief.
That after speech goes, still breathing, seeing
and listening might stay.

That to mention selling the house caused tears.

And each of us, that we are not the body,
exactly, and yet through the skin, eyes,
hair, we love.

That the clothes are not the person, nor objects,
books. Memory is the fixative.

There she moves. There she stops breathing.

Radiantia

Now after rain, now after lashing rain through
yesterday afternoon and into the evening,
now after rain, heavy at times, the leaves

tipped down on the scrub tree, junk tree in front
of me, volunteer growing out of the leaf pile,
the pile where we toss yard waste, where once

a primrose sent roots down, burgundy petals,
golden eye, now the branches weighted so much,
like fishing line when you add gray lead weights

Now after rain and no sun, the whole sky
a soft white gray, now after a soaking rain, sleep,
no sun, we make amends, try living

with each other without rancor, not as easy
as rain that drenches in a most universal way
sun drops just opened, trailing blue lobelia

at the window box's front, rain for invasive
species that we are trying to kill, for astilbe,
the last of the mayapple, first of tomato plants

standing tall in black dirt, and I find once
again astonishment in the small, breathe in,
breathe out, two suet cages hung for birds

The End of Grief

When red oaks have gone to sticks, when full
     summer has scorched us and we lie
satiated, sweat-salty, tired of feasts and yet
     still green, ready for the stripping down—

When the flocks have come through, in clouds,
     cedar waxwings with their bold masks—
delighting me, not singing but feasting,
     gulping mulberries, in the leafless time—

When the season turns and what we glimpse
     ahead is almost welcomed—
season's death, ours too, then I'll let her
     go, dear one, I'll close my rent heart.

Rowing American Lake

Telling a friend how my father stayed calm
through broken bones, accidents, fish hooks
caught in his hat, thumb, or his right palm—

the girl trying to cast was me, my books
set aside for American Lake, a rowboat.
He teaches me to row silver water, and he looks

casual about it. "Pull each oar and keep us afloat.
Pick a point on the shore, aim toward it."
I tremble even now, hearing the gentle note

love brought into his voice. Never a fit
when I blanched facing the wriggling worm,
a jagged cut. At work, he'd taken first aid—"Just sit

right there, and breathe deeply." His words, a germ
of wisdom, always. Where do I look,
my father gone, to find that? Middle of the term

when the blues wail out our losses in snow-
melt and rain-drift. Other people's parents
lying down for the last time. Stay calm, row.

At the Burke Lake Banding Station

It's as simple as nets
              hung between trees
         nets of such a fine gauge
they hang invisible. . . .

Migrating warblers and other
              woodland birds
         quickly tangle in them—
volunteers go out, unsnaring wings

and tails, slipping each flyer into
              a cotton drawstring bag
         coming back this Sunday morning
with more than fifty bags—

to be hung on a wooden rack
              with pegs, as though
         you'd hang up your keys or hat—
fifty struggling chirping bags.

The scientist working at a table
              takes out each bird,
         measuring, weighing,
blowing on its skull and breast

to assess body fat, calling out
              numbers to a guy
         writing it all down—
before she asks who'd like

to hold a veery, or a vireo,
           a Cape May warbler, or a black
      throated blue, a thrush,
a golden-cheeked one,

and at the end, each bird stands
           stunned on an open palm
      before leaving our table, tent,
circle for a migration route

south across forests, wild seas,
           a journey none of us
      have made, or could—
the veery weighs one point one ounce.

New Year: The Lustrous Owl

1.
Astringent light, freezing rain.
The tax man ahead. The deep reckoning.

2.
Birds seen, books read, miles walked.
There's an app to keep track.

Why are owls so elusive? Heard,
but not seen.

3.
Sky drips water that coats pine needles.
Sticky as pitch. That front-yard fir,

the stuff golden like syrup on your hands.

4.
Birdbath filled with oak leaves.
A frozen stew.

5.
My sister picking at a blanket,
my sister's legs climbing the railing of the bed.

6.
Comparison is the thief of joy.

7.
The lustrous owl is not a species
but an artist's rendition.

Black eyes, golden-tipped feathers.

8.
Eight in a row. A shooting gallery.
One goes down.

The county fair: chaos of sights, smells.
Cotton candy, grease of popcorn.

Ticket stub torn in half.

9.
I dreamed she was a skull on the floor.
The dog wanted to sniff—

no, I jerked the leash.
Jean was on her knees scrubbing,
scrubbing.

10.
Unwind the lights from the trees.

11.
In the front yard, swinging from the magnolia,
planetary balls—

my favorite: gold—

there is also crimson, citron.

12.
Snow tops them.
Ice will cause them to fall.

13.
Be prepared with an alternative heat source.

14.
A remote eye—we watched the end.
The same blanket

pulled up over her head.

15.
No other year but this, the one behind
not yet fading.

And this one? A dream swirling to shape.

16.
In another one, she called to me.
I stepped into a shallow boat—

And motion took us.

Stippled Leaf, No Trout

It was underfoot, a stippled leaf.
I could imagine a trout's flank, rosy scales.

Leaf-fall before snow in Michigan, before rot.
The fallen color underfoot, a riot of crimson.
Then burnt gold lying near the cottonwood, then broken bark.

Everywhere I stepped, I thought of her—
no longer able to drive, to walk alone.

A crew planted saplings, Tilia americana redmond.
I stopped counting at twenty-five, six.
I was imagining next summer, the leafing out.

Here stood each sapling dug in deep, with a circle
of mulch, a yellow label clasping a branch.

I went on trying out sentences in my mind,
I was trying out a landscape without her.
Under the linden trees where I will walk.

See, that is why sometimes a vandal breaks
a tree, snaps it in half as a cry—I get it now.

Not without my sister, not without her,
you will not grow up tall shading the field
where people come for a picnic, summer dusk.

It wasn't a trout's flank, not rose stippled across scales
but blood red spots on leaf and leaf, leaving mortal signs.

Dragon Jar

I never wanted to be that fat
with child—don't ask me

how I knew—trusting my gut
in my late twenties due to a dream.

Pale celadon, this, and Korean. I've been
to Seoul, bending to pick up a piece

of crazed greenish pottery in a garden bed
outside the National Museum. We're all

fragments—my dream featured someone
writing in a car window's fog,

letters spelling the word *aim*. See, the jar
stands with swelling sides, an underglaze

of iron brown, from the Yi
Dynasty, and the dragon's coils seem

snakelike. Note how, near the head, it's wearing
either a topknot or a beard. From the dream

on, she crafted a life of her choosing, each day
another dish steaming from the table. Maybe now

I could explain to my mother, she
of the dragon breath, "Oh love, it was never

about you!" And the storage jar held what,
you say? Water, or more luckily, some wine—

and often, of those departed, ashes, purified bone.

Near Auvillar: Chagall's Moissac Window

Color of the fields in August, russet, rust.

The teasel gone to seed, leaves become spikes.
Sun drops, moth mullein, black-eyed susan
with its dark serious eye.

I had stepped into the church out of the rain,
touching a hand into the dry font before crossing myself,
surprising an old motion—
                    hand making a cross on the body.

Feeling the ends of pews, I glided forward,
dipping my head, making a left turn
into the side chapel.
                    The painting was placed
low, in a thick stone wall. Lead seams ran
at angles, taking nature's journey
                    of no straight lines.

And that was all—darkest at the edges,
at the top and bottom—
                    fluff, down, seed
coming apart as I watched. The truth not
a chiseled stone or commandment
                    but a skewed window
etched with earthen tones.

Acknowledgments

My grateful appreciation to the following journals, whose editors were first to publish the following poems, sometimes in slightly different versions:

About Place Journal: "Sword Fern"
Asheville Poetry Review: "Stippled Leaf, No Trout"
Atticus Review: "Aerodynamic," "Balance, January," "Radiantia"
The Boiler: "Where Rivers Cross"
Cimarron Review: "The End of Grief," "Frontal View of Trees"
Coal Hill Review: "My Sister's Earth Day"
The Collagist: "Vertigo"
Connotations Press: "The Canopy"
Dunes Review: "Cottage at the Lake: Two Views," "My Aberglaube," "Nakedness, Spared," "Shadow of the Lightning-Struck Tree"
Indianola Review: "Knives on the Irish Air"
Kenyon Review: "The Slit"
Michigan Quarterly Review: "Fig, Strawberry"
New England Review: "Artisan"
Nimrod: "My Sister's Hand in Mine" (as "Mudflats, Heron")
North American Review: "Come My Cantillations"
Old Northwest Review: "After the Ice Storm," "After *The Lunchbox,*" "Stippled Leaf, No Trout"
One Trick Pony Review: "Near Auvillar: Chagall's Moissac Window"
Phi Kappa Phi Forum: "Goodbye to the Poetry of Marble"
Pirene's Fountain: "Pierced"
Plume: "Clark," "Double Vision"
Prairie Schooner: "Lamentation"
Salamander: "Milkweed Pod"

Santa Clara Review: "The Prodigal Daughter"
Southern Humanities Review: "Hardwoods"
Superstition Review: "Rowing American Lake," "Treatise on
      the Double Self"
Valparaiso Poetry Review: "After Lightning"

"*Dragon Jar*" appears in *Plume Anthology 4,* edited by
      Daniel Lawless (MadHat, 2016).
"*Columbus Day Storm*" and "*New Year: The Lustrous Owl*"
      appear in *Plume Anthology 5,* edited by Daniel
      Lawless (MadHat, 2017).

Thanks to my colleagues across campus at Grand Valley State University and especially in the Writing Department and the Department of Art and Design for their encouragement of my work. And for friendship, support, feedback and more from Martha Bates, Dick Thomas, Diane Wakoski, Michelle Boisseau, Marilyn Kallet, Alice Friman, Tom Aslin, Albert Garcia, and Stanley Plumly. Also, thanks to the Cool Women book group (you know who you are!), to my family, and especially to Stan Krohmer, first and best reader, my heart, and a steady presence with a painterly eye. Thanks for the cover art. Finally, thanks to Diane Lockward for selecting my manuscript and giving it a home at Terrapin Books.

About the Author

Patricia Clark is the author of four volumes of poetry, most recently *Sunday Rising*. She has also published two chapbooks: *Wreath for the Red Admiral* and *Given the Trees*. Her work has been featured on *Poetry Daily* and *Verse Daily*, and has appeared in *The Atlantic, Gettysburg Review, Poetry, Slate*, and *Stand*. She was a scholar at the Bread Loaf Writers Conference and has completed residencies at The MacDowell Colony, the Virginia Center for the Creative Arts, the Tyrone Guthrie Center (in County Monaghan, Ireland), and the Ragdale Colony. Awards for her work include a Creative Artist Grant in Michigan, the Mississippi Review Prize, the Gwendolyn Brooks Prize, and co-winner of the Lucille Medwick Prize from the Poetry Society of America. From 2005-2007 she was honored to serve as the poet laureate of Grand Rapids, Michigan. She is Poet-in-Residence and Professor in the Department of Writing at Grand Valley State University.